Sing The Lord's Prayer with Orchestra

LOW VOICE IN G MAJOR

By
Albert Hay Malotte

Singer on the CD: John Marcus Bindel, bass-baritone

ED 4218

ISBN 0-634-08765-7

G. SCHIRMER, Inc.

DISTRIBUTED BY
HAL•LEONARD CORPORATION
7777 W. BLUEMOUND RD. P.O. BOX 13819 MILWAUKEE, WI 53213

www.schirmer.com
www.halleonard.com

Introduction

There is a curious story behind the original publication of Albert Hay Malotte's "The Lord's Prayer." Sheet music for single art songs, sacred songs and light popular songs were still common publications in the 1930s. Major publishers such as G. Schirmer received many hundreds of song submissions each year from hopeful composers. "The Lord's Prayer" was just such a submission. The chances for an unsolicited submission being accepted for publication were (and still are) very slim. For whatever reason, possibly because there was already a full publishing schedule of sacred songs, "The Lord's Prayer" landed in the rejection pile.

Out of nowhere an order came in from a Midwestern music store for 500 copies of Malotte's "The Lord's Prayer," spurred by an Ohio radio broadcast of the song. A frantic search revealed that there was no such publication. A resourceful, tenacious editor had a long-shot hunch barely worth exploring, but to be safe took a look at the songs submitted for review. It wasn't there. Taking the hunt one more unlikely step, the pile of rejected songs was checked. There, at the bottom of the stack, was "The Lord's Prayer." Had the secretary gotten that far in typing rejection letters, G. Schirmer would have missed out on what turned out to be the most famous American sacred song of the 20th century.

gratefully dedicated to my friend John Charles Thomas

THE LORD'S PRAYER

Albert Hay Malotte

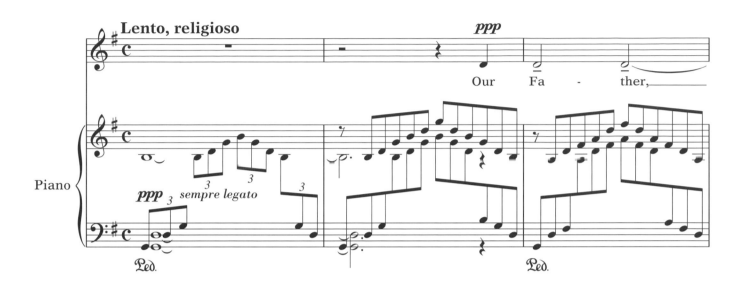

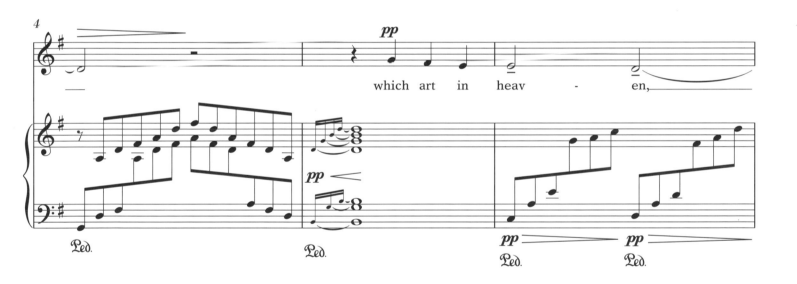

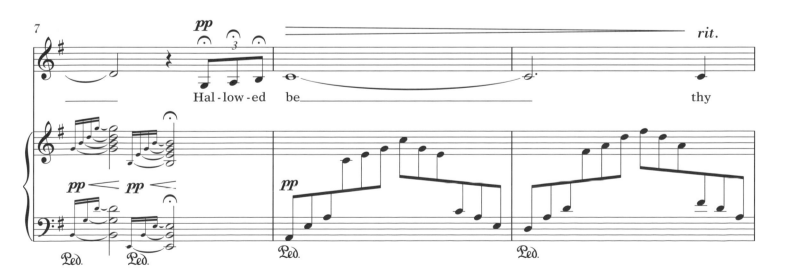

4

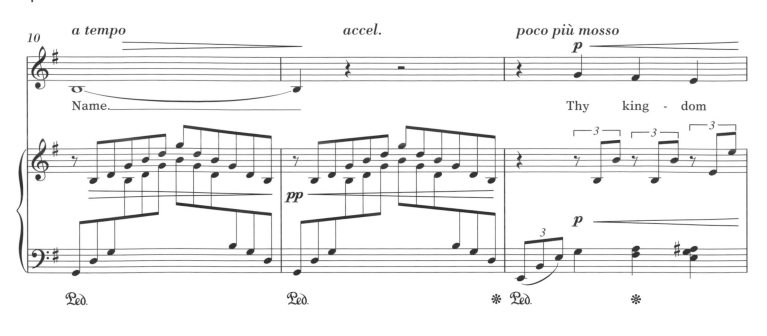

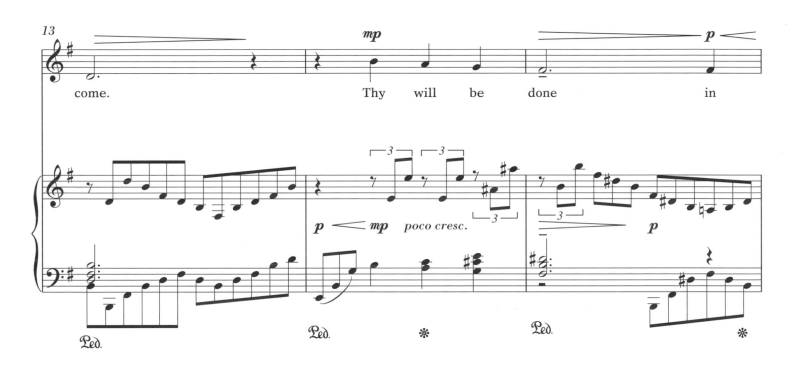

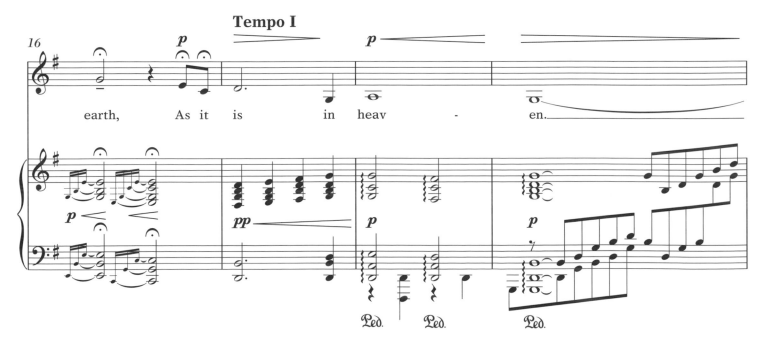

L'istesso tempo

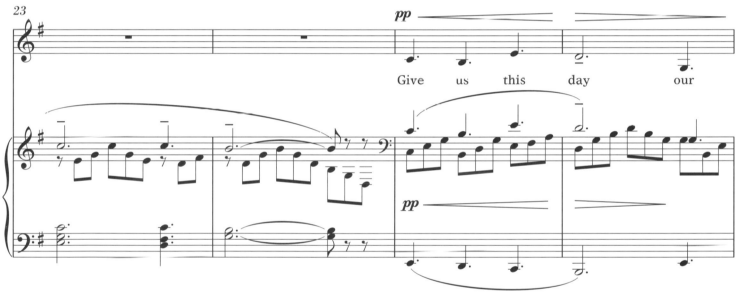

Give us this day our

dai - ly bread. And for-give us our debts,_____ As
tres - pass - es As

poco accel.

6

THE LORD'S PRAYER

Albert Hay Malotte
Organ Accompaniment
arranged by Carl Weinrich

Great *mf*
Swell *pp* to Great
Choir soft 8' 4'
Pedal soft 16' 8'

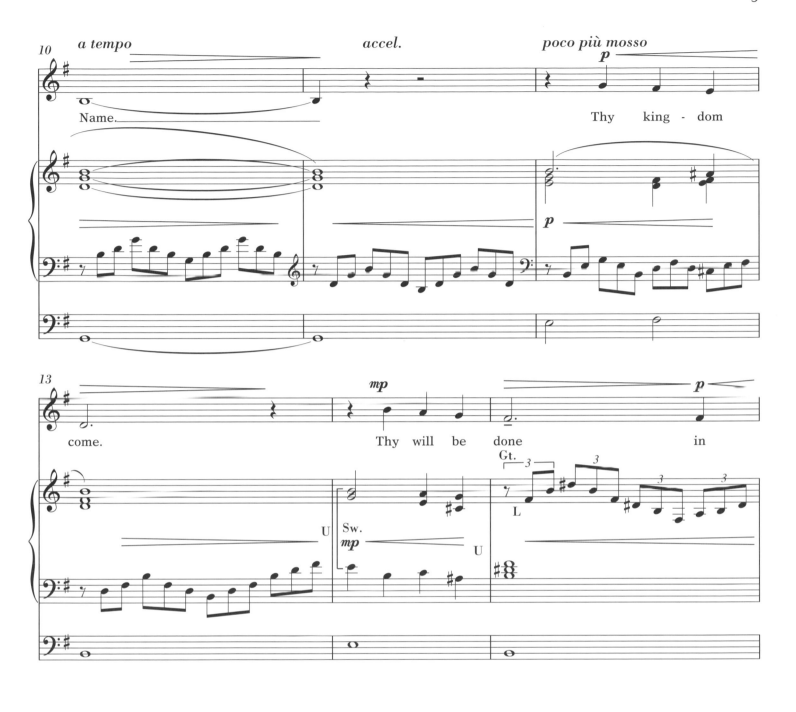

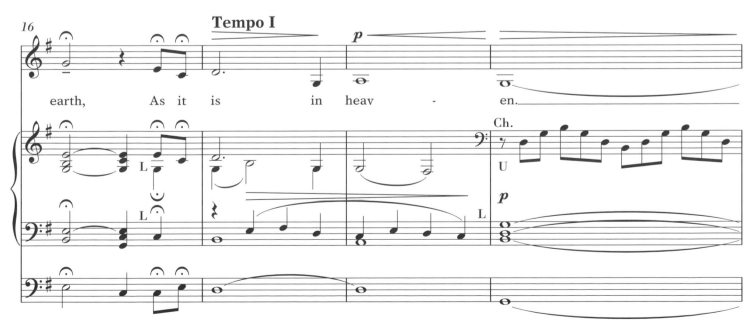